SMALL FISH
IN HIGH BRANCHES

poems by
ANNETTE SISSON

GLASS LYRE PRESS

Design & Layout: Steven Asmussen
Cover art: "Heron After Fish," Chris Stofleth
Author Photo: Rick Malkin

Glass Lyre Press, LLC
P.O. Box 2693
Glenview, IL 60025
www.GlassLyrePress.com

SMALL FISH
IN HIGH BRANCHES

This book is dedicated Jimmy Thomas Davis—
my partner in all of life's adventures,
and my sweetest love.

I am the daughter of earth and water,
And the nursling of the sky;
I pass through the pores of the ocean and shores;
I change, but I cannot die. . . .
I silently laugh at my own cenotaph,
And out of the caverns of rain,
Like a child from the womb, like a ghost from the tomb,
I arise and unbuild it again.

Percy Bysshe Shelley, "The Cloud," *Poems Written in 1820*

We find out the heart only by dismantling what
the heart knows. By redefining the morning,
we find a morning that comes just after darkness.

Jack Gilbert, "Tear It Down," *The Great Fires,* 1994

CONTENTS

Not the Happy Genius of My Household   1

1 LANGUAGE OF WATER

The Color of Light   5

The Amphibious Body   6

The Rain Spills   8

The Island Is Its Own Gospel   9

Cadence   10

Near Piccadilly   11

Sand Water Flower Sky   12

Prodigal Father   14

Straight from the Deeps of Stanley   16

Surface Tension   17

Charmouth Bay   18

2 CONFEDERATION OF WIND AND TREE

Poem   23

To See Small Fish in High Branches   24

Résistance   25

Learning to Read   27

The Mind's Ether   28

Figure of Song   29

Postcard from the Mother Ghost   30

Your Desire a Loaded Spring   31

Instinct for Touch   32

Hemingway's Head   33

Murmuration of Starlings   35

Crows Call, High Above the Floodplain   36

Birds and Trees, My Mother's Paintings   37

Fog   39

3 GRAVITY'S LEASE

Her Cosmos   43

Gravity's Lease   44

Magnolia   45

Leavings   46

Reckonings, 2019   47

Wind and Wildflowers, Edinburgh   49

Kitchened   50

A Honeyed Sorrow   51

My Keen and Doleful Heart   52

Lament for a Brother   53

Silver Links   55

December   56

The Scant Offices of Coffee   58

4 MORE THAN FIRE

Summer 1968   63

Metal and Glass   64

Cold to the Bone   65

Reflection #1: The Light That Covers Her   66

Reflection #2: What Rope Is For   67

In Pursuit of Starlight   68

The Thing Itself   69

Combustible   70

Eclipse   71

More Than Fire   73

CONTENTS

Not the Happy Genius of My Household   1

1 LANGUAGE OF WATER

The Color of Light   5

The Amphibious Body   6

The Rain Spills   8

The Island Is Its Own Gospel   9

Cadence   10

Near Piccadilly   11

Sand Water Flower Sky   12

Prodigal Father   14

Straight from the Deeps of Stanley   16

Surface Tension   17

Charmouth Bay   18

2 CONFEDERATION OF WIND AND TREE

Poem   23

To See Small Fish in High Branches   24

Résistance   25

Learning to Read   27

The Mind's Ether   28

Figure of Song   29

Postcard from the Mother Ghost   30

Your Desire a Loaded Spring   31

Instinct for Touch   32

Hemingway's Head   33

Murmuration of Starlings   35

Crows Call, High Above the Floodplain   36

Birds and Trees, My Mother's Paintings   37

Fog   39

3 GRAVITY'S LEASE

Her Cosmos   43

Gravity's Lease   44

Magnolia   45

Leavings   46

Reckonings, 2019   47

Wind and Wildflowers, Edinburgh   49

Kitchened   50

A Honeyed Sorrow   51

My Keen and Doleful Heart   52

Lament for a Brother   53

Silver Links   55

December   56

The Scant Offices of Coffee   58

4 MORE THAN FIRE

Summer 1968   63

Metal and Glass   64

Cold to the Bone   65

Reflection #1: The Light That Covers Her   66

Reflection #2: What Rope Is For   67

In Pursuit of Starlight   68

The Thing Itself   69

Combustible   70

Eclipse   71

More Than Fire   73

NOT THE HAPPY GENIUS
OF MY HOUSEHOLD

after William Carlos Williams, "Danse Russe"

How can I be lonely? A jar
of peach preserves makes its entreé
on a kitchen shelf among the pepper

mill, honey pot, mortar and pestle.
A bottle of Spanish wine flanks
a bowl of fruit, slack-skinned,

beside onions, sweet potatoes.
Sprigs of ivy root in a window-
ledge glass, and peace lily,

orchid, cyclamen peck at the pane
as if to inspire the outdoor garden
with their fancy blooms. The house

settles. Not born for loneliness,
I write. Aim for work that matters.
Flaunts its *is*-ness, flails its limbs,

dances too rashly on the page
to regard its loins—to notice the fouetté's
lift of leg, wild spin.

It abandons barre and mirror, struts
out to the paper's edge, greets
the viewers, who matter, their ripostes

flinging the work into flame-white *is*.

1

LANGUAGE
OF WATER

THE COLOR OF LIGHT

Water ripples. A translucent film
        creases itself into bright
    silk folds trailing the surface.
This color is no color. Nor
        transparent. It magnetizes the eye,
    a girl coveting jewels—
it must be the color of light.
        These distilled particles
    crystallize on Radnor Lake
early morning, sundown. They crest
        the western waters and cloud-
    shine over canyons. They glitter
in the Tetons' ice. The gibbous moon,
        the crescent, gleam—not white,
    not silver. As when we canoe
through schools of iridescent trout,
        revel in their didoes, sudden slices.
    As when you sidle up
to my back while I write at my desk,
        your slow breath in my hair, fingers
    on my neck, mouth over my ear.
Your nearness, graze, your astonishing
        fidelity, familiar as the melt of afternoon
    sun, as startling, as diaphanous, as the mist
of a waterfall's aura, as Radnor's dazzling
        glister, as a trout, its exuberant
    rainbow scales leaping into light.

THE AMPHIBIOUS BODY

I.

Off the road a cow lowers herself
into ditchwater, relieving the day's
weight and heat. Her body shrinks
as she curls her legs. *Leviathan*, I think,
and watch the highway dissolve
in a shimmer of dreamwater. . . .

II.

Two summers ago we launched
pontoons on an Indiana reservoir,
its shores austere, withering
from a three-month drought.
Our group of thirty stared
into sky, sure the air would vaporize
the lake. But we dropped anchor
at midpoint. I dragged my hands
in the drab water, observing
how it cleared over my fingertips.

III.

The water lapped the vessel,
air stirred—nothing like a zephyr,
or humidity dispersing. Simply
the indolent atmosphere ventilating,
somehow easing itself. We climbed
from the boat to bathe in the lake,
pushed against waves, yielded—
moved through water, tresses
uncoiled, the swell arranging
the plaits into wafting fans on an olive
drape. We looked below the surface
to see that our bodies blurred

into wavy lines, fingers faded,
arms and legs incandescent, merging
with the others' nebulous parts.

IV.

What, what would it mean
if we remembered how as children
our bodies were the language of water?

V.

I dream, a slow drowning—
watch the body descend,
long hair swirling around the head.
Nothing tugs or pushes; gravity
simply prevails. The self dissipates,
bones settle. There is no mourning.

VI.

When in daylight water encircles
my waist, I cannot stop checking
to see if my feet are still there.
If the outlines are faint, my thoughts
turn to seaweed, shale, undertow.

THE RAIN SPILLS

All evening the rain spills through the trees.
I think of the water as silver yarn,
the skein unraveling, threading its way

to earth. Falls of droplets pummel
leaves, confound the loamy soil.
The drumming eases. Sounds layer

the night, its jet mantle unfurling—

cicadas, frogs reverberate from a creek
bed, the faint grumble and shriek
of train cars, a truck engine buzzes,

a dog's yelp, another's bay.
I listen to how sound arrives in waves,
how it girdles the vibrating dark,

rhythmic like starlight—like image

knitting tone to form or figure,
lit by the mind, its fictive eye, alive.
Is the life beyond this life vision

or sound? Or the slate silence
before an idea forms: the first purl
of indelible rain, lengthening, gathering

heft, the hallowed fall into night?

THE ISLAND IS ITS OWN GOSPEL

The priory's jagged Celtic
walls stretch and yawn
as if aroused from Cuthbert's
ageless sleep. These
soaring ruins lord
over holy Lindisfarne,
islanded at high tide,
offering its quiet pages
to a seizing world.

There is no silence
like the chant of waves.
Drone of endless blowing.

Every outcropping of rock,
knee-high shoot
of marram grass, gray cloud's
sun-shimmered edging
reaches back to the mainland,
rolls through the burial
grounds. The island's immaculate
tongue, like eighth-century
monks copying a brilliant
sacred text: the ancient
pulse of these breathing
shores, their vibrant dead
wringing the north wind,
silence etched on vellum.

CADENCE

The tide rises slowly.
Water rolls and heaves,
pilfering layers of sand

from the inconstant edge.
And I recall your devotion
to an eastern sunrise, the chill

of the Charles, the Atlantic's pull.
Over wires and states
our conversation faltered,

its patter flattening like surf.
This break is the ache in the base
of my thumb, cartilage thinning,

scrape of bare bone.
It hovers like dust
in the corners of my bedroom,

mingles with dog hair
behind the closet door,
glints like limestone

in the garden, the path curving
away from the front porch.
It appears in my rearview

mirror, climbs into
the passenger seat through the open
window in springtime.

This breach lifts me softly
like the swell of an ancient sea
erasing the shore, swallowing its leavings,

its breakers the cadence of loss.

Near Piccadilly

homage to Jack Gilbert, "Married"

First Christmas, twenty-six years
ago, time tumbled ahead of us.
One day after, I boarded a plane
for London. Without you. Snow piled

along glittering streets. Wind blistered my eyes.
The Thames blustered, hushed by edgings of ice.
And every hour, my body missing its ribcage.
Heart valves slipping. I scoured the city

for relief. Traffic flooded the street, surged
from the wrong direction. I stood on a curb
near Piccadilly Circus straining to cross,
to gather myself, salvage the lost body

parts. Raw, blasted by river and gust,
hobbled by a cold ocean. Riven by want.

SAND WATER FLOWER SKY

after Hannah Cole, "Sea Mist and Poppies"

A painting: band of long-stemmed
poppies, pinks and reds, with blue-
purple cornflowers, whiffs
of sea grass. There must be a sun

here, angling from behind the viewer.
Bleaching two-story beach
houses white, tincture of pink
on roof lines, pinking white

sand that tugs gray seawater
flushed, sighing. Harbor boats,
grays and whites pinked by dots
of morning sun. Beside these

tracings of pink, hardly there,
the poppies seem to drain the color,
draw it to themselves, as if it all
comes down to flowers and light.

Let me begin again, focus
on the whole, its amplitude:
sky and sand, breath and ground,
water gliding toward passage,

tall grass and flora binding
earth, deflecting claws of rain.
Though the flowers' color-shine
seems too dazzling, too

charged with allure, without hue
and profusion the world is an orphan,
jailed in a crib, fed and diapered
by the clock, without touch, without

surprise, or play, or glee. And then
the world is a man, his eyes fixed
on his childhood's slivers, unfit to cast
beyond the shallows to where the parts and pieces

merge. A man who cannot say *love*
to his wife, whitewashes her days, her stinted
heart. A woman who gathers pearls,
lifts them to sunrise, lets them wash

away. In this famished life, even
sea oats, swept by currents
of water and wind, cry out:
sand water flower sky.

Prodigal Father

He stopped at every dam from Boise to Spokane,

curved through two-lanes of rock and scorched
dirt. Spirit Lake, Nine Mile,

Grand Coulee, Upriver, the rugged feats

of Big Sky and Great West. He downed
32-ounce beers, reeled into gas stations

for more, wrangled his wife, sparring over

the turns, the fastest route to the next dam.
Still, his voice sweetened as he stared at each

new edifice, rehashing design, construction—

the segment of river, its history, bed, channels,
how its topography must be taken to account.

Too, his kindness: When he spoke of the son

in Spokane, a half-way house, a judge's grace.
Understand his story, his sorrow. A good boy.

Such pressure. It's all about scaffolding.

This father, his sons, his beer and smokes,
acres of roiling lake, restrained, like the one

he girded up, held in with deep

footings, story, pylons of grit. His life
a tender architecture of need. That day

we spotted a stray runnel at the Coeur d'Alene.

It slid down the prodigious barrier, darkening
the rifts of baked red clay—not a burst

of rolling force, but a swill, a soft breach.

Straight from the Deeps of Stanley

The Sawtooths' jutting spikes, batholithic rock,
cut and bend the wind like scissors curling ribbon.

The stark, hard quick of their steeps calls,
and I am twenty-four again, when Idaho first

unfolded its simmering heart to me—cobalt plumes
of sky, silver lakes, whorls of glittering stars.

I drank deep from this cup. I baptized myself
in hot springs fogged by stiff night air.

Nine seasons of returning, renewing, summer revival.
Then thirty-three years of exile. A seismic shock.

No fault, no blame. A crack, a fissure. A continental divide.

This reunion is slate-bottomed cumulus bright
with muted lightning. Idaho peels back my skin,

opens me like a fish pulled straight from the deeps
of Stanley, the Sawtooths' giant escarpments peering down,

wading in, doubled. They break across
the silver-saged valley, clamber up

my spine, pierce me with the barbs of their crown.
Their shelves abide in the dark heart of a blazing

sun, their shadow a veil catching on my step.

Surface Tension

Water striders walk
           on fluid skin, feet
faintly bending surface,
            push-back propelling

them forward. Their pads press
            visible dents into the lake's
glaze, ingrained on the retina's
            membrane. This is not

a miracle. Still. If humans
            walked on water, would
we ever opt to swim?
            And if we scurried barefoot

across the liquid rind, molecules
            clumping before each footfall,
would we, at the lake's deep
            center, think our questions

answered? Would bullfrogs replace
            the call to mystery? Would
brain lose its skill
            for beyond, eyes cease

to measure depth, or even
            see a strider's surface
imprint as it skims for the slightest
            mite, as brief, as tense, as an inkling?

CHARMOUTH BAY

Ravens darken this cerulean
bowl, its lip a slender
pebbled strand. The Char's
estuary bends round,
rises into shelves of Jurassic
cliff, a mausoleum bearing
its dead back to sea.

In the fly-speck village
a lone parish churchyard
is laden with graves, modern
beside crumbling relics
askew. Mounds and markers
layer the eras, strata
of western clans guarding
their tight bonds, carrying
their freight of bones like spiny
furze gathered in baskets.

Beside the waves, the living
murmur into sinking light.
Brooms of cloud smear
evening's sky with rouge.
Young boys stalk
hermit crabs that skitter
to the deeps, take shelter.
The dwellers, with their fishing nets
and intricate webs of kin,
shelter too beneath
Charmouth's outcroppings,
ammonites spiraling
across a rocky beach,
as if they scorn the town's
accretions of dust, as if

they fathom the ocean's thrust,
brush of briefest eelgrass
by an ageless purling sea.

2

CONFEDERATION OF WIND AND TREE

POEM

The entrance must be fetching—
solid yet aged, peeling
so what's below almost shows.
Its hinges should heave and creak
but the oil can waits near.
Tall windows, curtains
pulled wide, usher in
errant flashes of sun.
Hardwood hums in the light.
All internal doors, unshut,
must surely lead somewhere,
perhaps a closet stacked
with hand-stitching—
pillowslips, a girl's apron,
fine books. Or maybe a long
hall, or frowzy vestibule.
The room may be furnished
in English garden, or vintage
yacht, or hermit's hut.
A writing desk cloaks
itself from visitors as if
a bureau drawer or strip
of wallpaper. As if it's not
a flight of stairs climbing
to a porch that opens
on a glade of saplings
and a sycamore wreathed
by late sky, an invisible wren
spilling tune into dusk.

To See Small Fish
in High Branches

My eyeballs' curvature feathers the forest.
I choose precision binoculars,
barium glass crisping texture and edge.
This crystal amplifies the air's flux
of lumens, gathers them up
like stray contours and plumes.
A bird forms in bouquets of light.

Without prisms, I see hawks
circle a blue afternoon, their tails
ablaze; a yellow-mauve iris,
the veins of its beard geometric
etching on sepal; the fluttering hem
of a cloudy lake; the startling girth
of a heron's nest lofted in sycamore.

The heron nestlings call for glass.
Its mesmeric gaze. To pierce the sky,
to see the heads bob, the parents'
talons, their powder down, the blue-
grey vigil as they tend the glossy
chicks—nebs, and tongues, and glints
of small fish in high branches.

Résistance

A red balloon wafts
          over a paddock of horses
near Haworth. It lifts
                    on bursts of air that reverse,
     push it groundward.
          It ascends again, larks
above the animals' heads
     like a gamboling kelpie.
                    Only one mare,
               blue-black, looks up,
                         inquires, bewitched.
     The balloon swoops. The mare
bolts, snorts, hooves
               the air, electrified. The orb
               rises again, cascades
          again, charming her,
                    luring her in.
It darts too close,
               she dips, tearing and bucking,
     and the scene loops, as if
          the players have forgotten the cue
               to unlock the script's sequence.
     A stalemate of horse and balloon,
                         of fear and curiosity. This
palpitating tension,
          this résistance.

* * *

25

Or, an inverse:

How

branching   saplings   in
a   perfect   biosphere
collapse   under   their
own   weight   seven
years   hence.   Regardless
of   variety.   Over
and   over.   No
wind.   Nothing   to
              withstand.

Like oblivious
mares pulling
up grass, gnaw-
ing lemony
clover. Like a
tree, too well
protected, sapped
of strength. Like
a life without
ballast, too fallow
to seed, too hollow
to bear wind, to
prod, to resist.

LEARNING TO READ

Not the breathless sprint home
after I bolted down a slick-wet
slide, body thunking ground,
a mud ball stomped flat.
Lungs knocked loose, vacuum
of air: This moment, not a page
in the book, but a child's rash panic—
flash of that blinkered last gasp.

Not a classmate's meningitis, fatal,
before the buses resumed their late
August routes. Nor even Kennedy's
brain exploding the air waves
three months after. The chapter
that carried these dead, graceless
in its heavy sheaves, seemed to me—
a young girl—spare and light,
ghosts to be swindled, outrun. Even
a ravaged uncle, chestnut eyes
sealed, slack mouth sutured
shut—for me, at thirty, he lingered,
winked, whispered, his page a loss
only my mother could parse.

When the chapter engraved with her name
arrived—*Mary Esther, Mom, Mimi*—
I watched closely, watched it absorb her,
become her. She pressed it to her chest
like a child, studied its sequence, held
it open. Her body collapsed into the final
leaves. I squinted to read these pages,
trifocals firm on my sinking face,
skewing the words that erased her.

THE MIND'S ETHER

Even now, my senses blunder. Is wind
    or rain bustling at the window? How

can the ear divide sound? The rise
    and fall of my husband's questions slide

past my ear canal, cochlea sputtering
    ciphers to cortex. My voice, my daughter's,

their timbre as matched as camelia to peony.
    Turnip greens pepper the tongue

like arugula, walnut repeats the creamy
    pulp of pecan, I taste the earthy

chamber in the beet. Distinctions flatten
    in the brain. And my astigmatic vision

fuzzes woodland stumps into resting
    deer, turtle to rock. Forest

scuffles as one body, and sun
    singes my eyes to darkness. In death

I may float in the mind's ether, the senses
    falling away, lungs slighting

their pattern, breath loosening, thought
    rising in the brain, rising into absence.

FIGURE OF SONG

A high-wire finch
plots his tones,
a five-point graph.

Orion migrates,
its turning a refrain,
figure of song.

If wind were silent,
would my tumbling
hair, the shuttering

lid against my pupil,
disquiet you?
Night sky points

in every direction,
paths of rhythms,
soundless intervals,

vibrations like chords.
A chaos of maps.
You are the hastening

air raucous
in my ear, a birdsong's
inflection of stars.

POSTCARD FROM THE MOTHER GHOST

Hammer yourself a ladder.
Lean it against the familiar,
and climb like deep-rooted
squash vines through daylight
and blue-white heat.
Rise into twilight, its pockets
emptied of fireflies. Do not
worry that you'll vanish,
that you're alone. Let
the ladder lift you beyond
the heavy face of night.

Turn the postcard over.

See the peonies I've brushed
into bloom, how they curve
like hands. In the pale life
that comes, there is no
climbing—only the heart's
circulation of time and desire.
Only a sweep of words,
sheen of petal and leaf,
the way dandelion fuzz ascends—
the way it doubles back, like prayer.

Your Desire a Loaded Spring

Your eyes drift west. I feel the distance
rise. The driveway cracks are widening,
the sagging bookshelves undusted
in the half-vacant bedroom that was yours.

Did I tell you, the vocal cords of Sandhill
Cranes measure five feet, their bodies
just three? The cords coil like
French Horns, their stentorian bugles
rattling for miles. Their bodies, lithe
and strong-legged—ballerinas with scarlet
turbans—seem hardly able to contain
such freight, to emit such cries.
And the corkscrews inside, the springs
that propel their flight, wings unfurling
as they leap, heads pumping low.

Last May I heard the Sandhills' call.
As they launched, clamoring high above
the marsh, becoming invisible, I saw your coiled
body, your desire a loaded spring. Your voice
is the overture before the dancers' buoyant cabrioles,
before the cranes' sacramental journey to the Platte.

INSTINCT FOR TOUCH

We wake. The owls
            convulse the woods below.
      Stiff as possums,
we lie on a rummaged
      mattress, the screened
            porch our answer
      to April's early swelter.
Their bellows, hoots,
      call and response,
            their instinct for touch—
      like our bodies,
sleep's arrival, even
      in heat's ruthless press,
            sheathed in barest gauze,
      brush of sheet on skin.

We long to touch
      the dead, loft words
      to dormant ears,
voices to clouds
      beseeching rain,
            its graze, thunder,
      its burst, antiphonal
rumble from the other
      side. We are owls
            coveting the dark
      echo of our need,
naked slumberers
      reaching for cover.

Hemingway's Head

A mound of flat rocks
stacked randomly
like a funeral pyre.
Modest tapered column
mounted on top.
Channel of water surging
past, its shallow stone
walls extending from
the dusky edifice.
His bronze head, no
shoulders, crowns the tower,
seems to float—serene—
in a stand of aspen.

He communes
with cottonwoods, trout
streams, granite scarps,
yellow autumn leaves,
white trunks with gray
pocks—a teal glass sky
blotted with pearl,
beyond comprehension.

Sun Valley, living
flesh of his colossal
desire, living flesh
of the withering bones
he relinquished—bodies
forth its deep quiet.
The elemental fact
of his head staring,
so intact, impervious,
estranged on that pillar,
as he surely was,

his brain bursting
into diamond shards
that cut the pristine sky,
the clouds agape, shrieking
shots of rain on dust.

Murmuration of Starlings

I.

A cancer spreads in the sky—
proliferation of a thousand cells
as masses of starlings mingle.
Wings froth the air,
a corpus boiling. Its protean
shapes flash from wasted
field to barren branch,
a rupture of fevered darkness
mounting in patterns of light.

II.

Myloma multiplies. Factory
workers disperse like smoke.
Damaged hearts choke
back blood. And I am
stained, blighted as pine,
recalling winter rye's
indelible skin, green
as chrysalis, as lacewing.

III.

The body rises, synchronic,
the birds feathered in.
The cloud of lift stuns.
Like exhalation after
siege, like a bruise,
like rapture.

CROWS CALL, HIGH ABOVE THE FLOODPLAIN

An empty wooden frame, years
layered like rings of oak, the painting
discarded—a turbulent sea and sky
scarcely divided, streaks of gray
mimicking a choleric body of water.

You consider a new canvas, how
it might be stretched, fitted—perhaps
a mossy kayak, a river, its creeping
tendrils and fronds jacketing mud-
slick banks. From the mullioned
window of a rural farmhouse, black-
slatted fencing bisects fields
of grass, rusty-feathered weeds.
Crows light in tree tops an acre
away. Jabbering ducks aggravate
the sky. A northern mockingbird scats
a rhyme, and coyotes shriek into night,
their scraping laughter sandpaper on slate.

Ducks spread their wings
on rivers of air—like paddles turning,
countering surge. The canvas beckons
these birds, this kayak bearing you
through woodlands, copper fields patched
with fencerows, crows calling from threadbare
trees high above the chalky floodplain.

BIRDS AND TREES,
MY MOTHER'S PAINTINGS

I ponder treetops to and from Indiana,

scanning them for hawks. Miles of bare
trunks splinter into shards, feather softly.

Dozens of hawks perch high. One

lands, a sweep of dark accordion fans
snapping closed beside a wide cream belly.

Muscular. Sturdy. Two Cooper's test

the smallest limb with their heft, the sag
and bend visible from the asphalt streaks of road.

My mother's paintings of trees lack birds.

She gave me four branching trunks in oil,
one of a scarlet tanager. None of both.

I want to ask her why. Maybe she struggled

with proportions. Maybe she confided in me
and I forgot to remember. I have waited

too long to inquire. Fixed in her recliner,

beyond words, she can no longer explain.
On the drive back to Tennessee, I search

again for trees with hawks, robust and alive,

wonder if the phoebes will appear this spring
to reclaim their nest in her front porch rafters,

re-build for a new brood. My mother

will be past knowing, staring out
into trees somewhere beyond the window

that opens to their labor. In the birds, the trees,

the way she feathered oil on canvas,
I will remember the phoebes, parents flying

off for insects, chicks' mouths gaping.

FOG

How the gray-white high rise
   diffuses into gray-white sky, the
     metal bones melding into cloud, as
if the hard lines quietly thinned
   as the steel expanded into vapor.
     How my mother's body loosens its hold

on earth and daylight, language
   and sense. How her hands that rise
     and jab at assailants in the blank air
still reach for a tissue, placing the
   box back on the table's edge, tenderly,
     how they wipe the rim of the bucket that

contains the retch of her dry
   heaves. How her wide eyes in the
     bones of her gray face fix themselves
on me as she says my name, her
   thin voice wailing "sorry, sorry,
     sorry." How can she know this lament

is my own? How can she reckon that
   her eldest daughter, the one she still
     remembers, would press her toward the
precipice, already pictures her rising
   into mist, seamless like girders, glass,
     and sky—gray-white bones vanishing in fog.

3

GRAVITY'S LEASE

Her Cosmos

They built a cottage
from the forest's growth,
consecrated it
through rituals of morning,
routines of seasons, leaves
dropping, budding, greening—
sealed by the thick mud
of their life's steep slog.

Now at dark he lifts
her from chair to bed,
sees the last of her
tomorrows emerge from the trees,
the deer gathered, grazing
in the front yard, nipping
the tips of the fig trees.

And he knows
when they come again
from the undergrowth,
rising from their wild
nests, come to taste
whatever new has grown,

she too will rise
carrying a loose bouquet
of cosmos, like those
she planted beside the porch,
some dropping silent
on grass, as she retreats
into mist and branches,
a veil of darkening shimmer.

GRAVITY'S LEASE

The rental house empty at last,
she bends to pluck a daylily
by the sidewalk, striped and gangly,
leaning to light, vestige
of her four-year stay. Heading
back home, back to her parents,
she stops to tighten the tether
on second-hand furniture in the pick-up.
An unexpected phone call: the dog's
passing, close of a slow circle.

She had claimed the white dog,
male, rescue, mutt of a certain
age. Her parents had bowed to her petition:
Two brothers, older, unclenched
her tightening grasp. The dog—
fair compensation for this breach
of gravity, cleft in the orbit of her will.

She buries the dog on the hill
of the back yard, the balm
of his presence. Shoveling,
she notices layers of silt and rock,
roots, gradients of color, sediment
accumulated with the earth's rotation,
the pull of gravity's lease.

MAGNOLIA

The magnolia's thick, brown leaves
cover all—
grass, weeds, sunflowers, pansies—
stacking up
like dirty laundry in the front yard.
A nettling presence.
The ones not fallen, rusty
leather against
a bright blue sky, are soon
impervious to brooms,
stuck in rakes. Heedless of our labors,
they half-bury
the small shoots we tend.

If its voluptuous blossoms
are spirit, incarnate
bodies of blooming breath, and the seeds
the life-force
of lung and heart, the pods are surely
the body, protective,
resilient, barbed. But the leaves,
neither body
nor blood nor breath, heave and strangle,
piling on
the fact of death. The spectacle
of lustrous white
flowers, the size of a baby's christening
gown, is no
compensation; it cannot atone. The seed
pods, hard
and sharp, cut bare feet,
blood as crimson
as the kernels stowed inside.

Leavings

My daughter,

A child of four, too soon,
you grasped that breath would pass,
that you, and we, would die.
You took in mortality, tended it
like a wound, like a garden.
You could not abide a listless tulip,
nor the morning's pattern of leaving.

Now it is late February.
You construct beds, curate soil,
plant kale, basil, favas, tomatoes,
a lemon tree in a clay pot—
witness stalks breaking through,
their sprouting, ripening, their leaving.

For each golden lemon plucked,
a white star once burned
with bitter zest. The tree's foliage
abides, greening all the year,
and you, steward of grief and seed,
consent to the constancy of soil—
the deep earth's lyric of leaving.

RECKONINGS, 2019

New Year's Eve.
Last late afternoon.
Crows squawk over bare
woods. Gray overcomes
the fainting pink of a brindled
sky, and I am counting:
coins, hours, luck,
costs. Gloaming distills
into sequined night, pulls
a new decade from its pocket.

Weeks before, I watched
Canada geese lift,
deserting the lake, a long
V rising, headed
where? Wings creaked
like old leather, a rhythmic
rasp. And then a shuffling
at the water's edge. Not
the lapping of waves, not
fish zagging, not
any animal. A sound
like the earth exhaling,
a deep whir for a hundred
yards. Maybe more.
I've walked that piece
in all seasons, mornings,
noontide, afternoons, dusk.
Never heard the like.

The new year will uncoil,
trail the far rim
of a tall bluff. What
strange noise may lure

me from this path I cannot
say. Coins are sorted,
fortunes cast. The earth
utters its secret churnings.
I count on loss, misgiving—
step into gleaming night,
hours leaking behind me
like gilded threads of dust.

WIND AND WILDFLOWERS, EDINBURGH

She climbs Arthur's Seat, photographs
the rocks, the harbor, the Medieval walls,

stills the rush of her solitude,
sharpens its telescopic lens.

A stolen day, its sweetness
as rare as rest, as winsome as Scottish

sunshine. Teetering on a shard
of granite, near the drop to meadows

of long grass swept horizontal,
she rides the cusp of summer,

basks in heather and gorse,
the next year a heart skip,

a sharp hollow breath. Tense
wind pushes her down, multiplying

gravity; she pictures not
the grey stones, but the dexterous

wildflowers, their purples, blues,
and whites cracking the sandy earth.

KITCHENED

The puppy idolizes windows.
On hind legs she paws
the low sill, scratching,

sniffing for breeze. Outside
a golden retriever lounges.
The little dog whines,

recalling the planes of the big
dog's back, her mouth
filled with wads of his fur—

she hankers to dangle from his pale
neck above the yellow clover.
I have stopped looking

out of windows. I am
kitchened, stifled in my mind's
house. Even in afternoon

light I stall at the garden
border. I am cabbage,
layers nested in.

Oh, to be cantaloupe,
to flower with insouciance,
vine into the next yard—

the fruit rough-surfaced,
celled with design, spilling
sweet seeds from the hollow inside.

A HONEYED SORROW

This return, as pressing
as autumn's bow to winter,

as binding as the confederation
of wind and tree. The cord

unraveled, I travel
to see again these lost

parents, wonder why
this pilgrimage, why

this abiding gratitude,
this need to part anew.

And the smell of autumn leaves,
overripe and brittle,

their decay a tender
savory—ligneous and piquant,

like dark chocolate,
its sweetness scarcely sweet.

This mud on my tongue,
not bitter—

the honeyed sorrow
of an aged and faultless earth.

MY KEEN AND DOLEFUL HEART

You threaded the machine,
wound the bobbin, set
the foot feed. I turned away
restless, young, indifferent.
Now I sort your stacks
of fabric, reach for a pattern.
I drink your raspberry tea,
copy your recipes, study
your paintings, journals, the weather
you recorded, the rain you measured.

These habits folded your days
into shapes, arranged by time
and color: red poppies,
white shastas, the emerald
swatch of a hummingbird's head,
moonshine on corn silk,
the loam that warms the stalks'
roots, their first rising.

I want you to know
how I mark the monarchs
and bluebirds, how I monitor gardens
and clouds, fields long with stubble,
how I gauge rainfall, the flowering
of blackberries—how I crave
your corduroy and flannel in October.
Your stitches are the measure
of my footfall, the bright constrictions
of my keen and doleful heart.

LAMENT FOR A BROTHER

When did the rib
of his small hope crack?
Was it split by the broken
woman fingering the creamy
divot where his breastbone
dips and latches, the delicate
hollow where a newborn
could burrow, where
his cantilevered ribcage
arcs, as if to lift
a child's lament—his own—
to the beating rise of day?

In the photo my brother,
age twenty-five,
hoists my infant daughter
fussing to his chest. Her head
bobs above his right
shoulder, eyes drift
behind him, yield
to the rhythm of his nestling.
Twenty-five years
later, home from work,
alone, he soothes his Balinese,
rakes its long fur,
rattles its fleshy belly.

In childhood he crammed
khaki pockets with toads,
wept for their maiming,
their crooked trusting leaps.
He cradled a still rabbit
in his shaking arms,
jostled it, grieving how

it leapt from his keeping
just before the garage
door thudded.

Silver Links

I examine the chain's silver links,
intact, mint condition, wonder

if my mother remembered this tender claim,
if she meant to tell me where to find it

before she fell silent. If she
recalled our dress-up dates,

our races to lap bowls of milk
on the kitchen floor, kittens on hands

and knees, Friday pizzas made
with hot dog disks and Colby,

the come-as-you-are parties on snow
days, tricycles overturned to churn

ice cream from clumps of new-mown grass,
doll clothes traced from wallpaper books,

talks late into nighttime with neighbors,
lawn chairs abutting the property

line, jokes about who had to clean
up the ashtrays, Coke bottles,

pickle jars of dead fireflies.

December

My mother waited until after
exams to reveal a fourth
child to be born in December.
At twelve, I wondered how
much more would be
expected of me, the other
two siblings clamoring
for my lap, small feral
cats squabbling for turf.
I knocked the screen door
off its frame, fled
to the dense trees behind
the house, silently ranted
at my mother, my mind a grenade,
a field of trip wires detonating.
I swore I would not help.
I would vanish from the household,
will myself into nothing.

At eleven, I'd thought to settle
into quiet sleep, my mother's
cancer finally purged,
our family a tender patchwork.
But time stretched like elastic,
its edges frayed, unraveling—
and the grief of pubic hair,
the twenty-year-old next door
smoking on his parents' carport,
the open bedroom window,
my sheet a welter of knots.

Each morning I choked
back December, staggered
outside. Some days

I slipped into dark shade,
quarreled with squirrels. Others
I mounted the blue banana
seat, peddled hard
up the long hills, careened
down, feet splayed.
I chased velocity and distance,
this daring an ache, a fury,
wildness of latitude. Once
I scraped rock, hurtled
over handlebars, landed
on barbed wire, face-
down on hot asphalt.
Summer sprinted ahead,
collapsed into fall, its bitter
brittle leaves—I couldn't
explode, or fade away,
couldn't bypass December.

THE SCANT OFFICES OF COFFEE

This meager accord,
a coffee mug empty

even when filled,
caustic as the liquid

inside. Outside
a red-bellied

woodpecker catechizes
the root of a maple,

its flint beak
at ground level

prying out ants
and bark lice.

You hear its drumming,
cannot see

its ruddy helmet.
Your barren eyes,

their sight vexed
and flat, the way

you've viewed me,
always. What can

this filial tie be?
Only a hollow

of want. Only
my father, unyielding,

fearful, dark
to the flame of a bird's

crown—shrinking
from me, assiduously

performing the scant
offices of coffee

too acrid to drink,
too measured to bear.

4

MORE THAN FIRE

SUMMER 1968

. . . I must start
Where things began to happen and I knew it.
"Ground Swell," Mark Jarman

Transistor radios popped
as I teetered on stilts,
a unicycle, a crazily painted
barrel unrolling my name
on yards of grass. From a thick
trunk laddered with slats,
I lofted myself into elm,
forks wedged with planks—
sat tall, drifted among serrated
leaves, imagined falling.

I submerged my body
in the dark deep of a creek
bend, made camp
under a heavy moon,
the night damp gauze,
crickets electric. I stowed
hard sours in slick
cheeks like plugs of tobacco,
my parents, creased at the brow,
hunched over newspapers,
Life magazine, photos
of body bags in long rows.

That was the summer
when the plastic horses
I liberated to graze
the front yard balked
at the porch's edge.
Cicadas—fire red eyes
and pulsing screams—
buzzed the leafy canopy,
spent shells clinging tight.

METAL AND GLASS

In the milky glass of sleep,
you dream of leading students

on a field trip to a place
you have no earthly idea

how to find. The memory's
metal barbs scrape

the delicate skin of morning.
What I want to tell you

is as upright and true as the white
cosmos in the front garden.

Their feathered stalks lean
into October wind, rain

coating the veins of blooms,
a thin platinum sheen.

Hear me: no one
ever knows anything

for sure. Every single
thing you've learned is your car

teetering on a mountain two-
lane, no shoulder,

a flatbed barreling toward you
targeting the windshield's glare.

COLD TO THE BONE

Boots, two pairs of socks, feet
cold to the bone. White sheers ruffling
at the window, register breathing softly.
Sun lifts the room into light.

I unzip the brogans, peel away
thermals like leaves from cornstalks—
extend bare toes to the pane,
poaching the warmth collected in glass.

My sister calls. And calls. In Indiana
the pack of snow is splotched, gray
with muck. It buries her sidewalk. Her busted
shovel can't take the weight of wet snow.

I buy teas, cat treats, pack a photo
of our mother stirring at a hot stove.
I wonder how to quell the chill,
deliver boxes of warm jellied toast,

pry hope loose like windshield ice,
send her a morning with arms like sunlight.

REFLECTION #1:
THE LIGHT THAT COVERS HER

after Edward Hopper's "Eleven A.M."

I have known this woman. How
    she stares out into day, into the vertical chasm
        between this building and the next, thinking.

She bends from the hips. Elbows and forearms rest
    just above knees, hands clasped.
        In a dark plush chair she angles

toward the window. Morning slants in,
    sheathing her pale nude body in gold.
        Loose auburn hair shades her shoulders

almost as if she were clothed. Black flat
    shoes mask her toes. She wears nothing
        more. Not a chemise, ring or barrette.

She mulls it over—studies its shadow and shine,
    ponders how sunset might alter its prospect.
        She will stand, move into time, into noon,

and after, as if she were stepping out of the room's
    chiaroscuro, through the window's low sash,
        stone chamber hard against her tilted form,

stepping into obliques of light that cover her.

REFLECTION #2: WHAT ROPE IS FOR

If she lived in this world,
no longer would she murmur
about her appetite for Wyoming—
rocks, feathers, an open hand,
a conjuring. Her desire
is flamingo, a train ticket
to Aberdeen, the shiny midnight
of Hollywood starlight on paper.
And Wyoming. What she has
is a campaign button, leftover
bread crusts, a length of rope
knotted in place, its other end
circling. If she clutches its swing,
perhaps abrading her idle
hands, then she might ride
the arc high, unfist her grip,
hurl herself into the tall
plains, range that wide
horizon, filling herself with the glint
of minerals, flash of kites,
the sated life of rock and feather.

In Pursuit of Starlight

I.

The astronomer's uncanny string
of numbers pinpoints the oldest star,
its yellowish-white light christened
cosmic latte. It originated thirteen
point eight billion years ago,
six thousand light-years away,
each light-year six trillion
miles. Earthbound, we study
curving mirrors to see what opacity
and desolation might yield,
our fathoming universally derived,
interpolated by a factor of cosmic dust.

II.

A man trains chimpanzees to explode
into space, streak through dark energy,
break into orbit. The compliant apes
manage levers, signal their waking,
their aliveness. They bow to the lure
of work, their ball-peen focus
a window in a dark vessel,
hypnotic as whirling hydrogen.

III.

Idaho's dark skies pull us
to its barren black. The indifferent moon
burns low. A slow nightfall mists
our breath, crawls into our jackets,
seeps under the hoods. When the stars
blink into view, as if just awakened,
we fall into sky, reckless of warmth
and ease. Stardust leaks into our pupils.
We are starlit from the inside out.

THE THING ITSELF

You tell me of your brother's
stroke, the sharp swerve
of his path. You will drive
all day to see him.
I want to join you,
to confide as we did in college
when life was a pointed question,
when raw feeling couldn't
walk a straight line.

Now life has been sanded
down for refinishing,
too dull to cast its spell,
too self-absorbed
to mark our craving for amazement.
We struggle to taste salt,
to weep for the thing itself.

Still, the years pulse
and spin, a helix, a curve
in space. And we risk
loving it, the fruit, pit
and all, as we exalt
in the wonder of breath, the story's
climax, the throb of loss,
the tang of summer's succulent
first ripe peach.

COMBUSTIBLE

Before the first touch, first
skim of tongue, I thought you
tame as a brother, thought winter
bereft of warmth. Then bonfires
      flared, bursting the jeweled air.

Now we wake side by side,
skin untouching, circulate the house
like soft heat. The thin smoke
of our orbit trails these rooms.
      Daylight lengthens, its slow burn.

We recall our bodies, crescents nested,
stirring the smoldering ash of night,
sheets murmuring moonglow—
strip away the day's parched crust,
      urge the amber coals to flame.

ECLIPSE

I.

The moon passes between Earth and sun,
its shadow crossing the crust of our lives.

History eventuates into now.
The sun shrinks, dies away—

dark's aperture swallows us
whole. This passing into blackness

completes itself in scalding light,
ringing the disk with torrid flame.

II.

A box truck stalls on the hill.
A dump truck tows a trailer up.

A pick-up above the box truck
begins to push it onto the trailer,

its tongue popping up from the cargo's
weight, the dump truck's back

wheels leaving the ground, brakes
helpless in mid-air. The box truck,

only half loaded, and the trailer,
the dump truck: all lunge downhill,

a forklift straight in their path, back
wheels and tongue still raised

high—a triangular cavalcade skidding,
sliding, dreadful behemoth on the lam.

III.

The son rushes to mount the dump truck.
His father hastens to the front, angles

his pick-up to halt the sliding mass.
Unable to see his son hurtling

for the door, he crushes him between dump truck
and pick-up. His son's body crumples

under the trailer. He is broken. The silence
is staggering, damage eclipses belief.

IV.

The piercing scream of metal on asphalt,
the father's lurch of knowledge, riot of gut.

His spiraling agony—cataclysm of seared
retina, sun effaced by a fractious moon.

This father treads a relentless crepuscular
earth. His light passes each morning.

The shroud slips over him, envelops
him, nullifies thought, seals him up.

MORE THAN FIRE

Fire slices the air, a neighbor's
brush pile wild with flame.

A storm bursts over the ridge
flinging tree limbs like cudgels,

power lines tied like twine.
The fullness of this evening descends.

I write by candle. Its flashing eye
pools light on my hand, shadows

the room's cavern, objects just shy
of their whole selves. That night

I awake, the high moon a flawless
ivory chalice. I consider its roundness,

paleness, the prospect of death, of dying,
strands of knotted breath untying,

letting go. I am not ready.
I flinch, confess *rain, wind,*

word, fire to the unbroken sky.
What compresses the chest when energy

slackens, when breath and oxygen fail,
is the brush fire's rampant blaze,

the flutter shadow light of desire,
the wind, vast and ambient, stilling,

condensing into less than a page can say.

NOTES

The following poems are dedicated to my partner, Jimmy Davis: "The Color of Light," "Figure of Song," "Reckonings, 2019," and "Combustible."

The following poems are dedicated to my daughter, Evan Davis: "Your Desire a Loaded Spring," "Wind and Wildflowers, Edinburgh," "Gravity's Lease," and of course "Leavings," which addresses her directly in its opening.

In "The Color of Light," Radnor Lake is part of Tennessee's first designated natural area.

"The Island Is Its Own Gospel" is written in response to "The Holy Island," also known as "Lindisfarne," on the northeastern coast of England in Northumberland. Although Lindisfarne can be accessed by land from the mainland most of the time, it becomes an island at high tide—about six hours each day. Lindisfarne was settled in 634 CE by the monks of Iona Abbey, located on the Isle of Mull off the west coast of Scotland.

"Prodigal Father" is written in memory of my first father-in-law, Dene Brock, who passed away December 4, 2020.

"A Honeyed Sorrow" is dedicated to Dene and Alice Brock, my first parents-in-law.

The following poems are dedicated to my mother, Mary Esther Sisson (4/19/1936 – 1/23/2018): "Birds and Trees, My Mother's Paintings," "My Keen and Doleful Heart," and "Silver Links." Several others are inspired by her and my experiences as her daughter.

Stanley Lake is located in the Sawtooth Mountain range in central Idaho.

"Charmouth Bay" is located in West Dorset county on the Jurassic Coast in southern England—a jot east of Lyme Regis.

In "Résistance," Haworth is a village in West Yorkshire, England—famous especially because the Brontë family lived there.

"Hemingway's Head" was inspired by The Hemingway Memorial on the edge of Ketchum in Sun Valley, Idaho.

"The Thing Itself" is dedicated to my dearest friend, Kimberly Burnett.

"Eclipse" was written in response to a tragic accident that occurred in front of our home, on a street tucked into a crevice of Forest Hills in south Nashville.

ACKNOWLEDGMENTS

I am immensely grateful to Glass Lyre Press—to Ami, Kelly, Linda, Steve—for selecting this book for publication and your support throughout the project. It has been an honor and pleasure to work with you, and I am humbled by your generous enthusiasm for bringing this book into the world.

I am deeply grateful to Belmont University for my Spring 2020 sabbatical, which enabled me to complete this book, and also for offering financial assistance for my attendance at Poets on the Coast, Sanibel Island Writer's Conference, and Rockvale Writers' Colony. All of these provided support, learning, and time for writing.

Thank you to The Porch Writers' Collective for awarding me their first annual Poetry Prize (2019) and for the many wonderful workshops through which I've had the pleasure to study with Bill Brown, Gary McDowell, Ciona Rouse, and Amie Whittemore—all wonderful poets.

I am grateful to Bill Brown and Jeffrey Levine who read this manuscript and provided encouragement and constructive feedback; your belief that it really was a book, as well as your suggestions and questions, helped me more than you know.

Thank you to Chera Hammons, Mark Jarman, and Kevin Stein (all poetry idols of mine) for agreeing to read this book and provide blurbs even though you knew little of my poetry. And to Kevin, thank you for sharing your knowledge and offering such helpful suggestions; I have aimed here to take your advice.

Many thanks to the "Daydream Believers" poetry critique group, as well as the women of Zalon and ZDD, who helped me refine several of these poems; I truly appreciate your friendship and feedback.

With deep love and gratitude to the many students, colleagues, Glendalers, and other friends who have cheered me along this path, helping me to believe—as George Eliot's life first showed me, and as my mother demonstrated—that "it's never too late to be what you might have been."

And I am grateful to Melody Wilson, who has become an indispensable friend and writing partner—a rare and rich find in this hurly-burly world of poetry.

Finally, endless appreciation to my partner Jimmy Davis, who has read every poem—from ridiculous first drafts to final manuscript—and offered me, at every step, his honesty and support, patience and enthusiasm, belief and love. Know this: This book could not have happened without you.

Publications

Thank you to the editors of the following journals, in which poems in this book, sometimes in earlier versions, first appeared:

The Blue Mountain Review, "Her Cosmos"

Coastal Shelf, "1968" (now "Summer 1968")

Cordella Magazine, "My Keen and Doleful Heart"

Front Porch Review, "Gravity's Lease"

Gyroscope, "Lament for a Brother"

Hamilton Stone Review, "The Color of Light," "A Honeyed Sorrow," "In Pursuit of Starlight"

HeartWood Literary Magazine, "Cold to the Bone"

Hole in the Head Review, "Not the Happy Genius of My Household"

KAIROS, "Hemingway's Head," "Magnolia"

Kissing Dynamite, "Instinct for Touch"

Kosmos Quarterly, "Sand Water Flower Sky," "Postcard from the Mother Ghost," "Kitchened"

Manzano Mountain Review, "The Light That Covers Her," "More Than Fire"

Meat for Tea: The Valley Review, "The Rain Spills," "The Place of Poetry" (now "Poem")

Nashville Review, "Fog"

Naugatuck River Review, "December"

One, "Your Desire a Loaded Spring," "Reckonings, 2019"

Orange Blossom Review, "Metal and Glass"

The Orchard's Poetry Review, "Wind and Wildflowers, Edinburgh"

Panoply Zine, "Silver Links"

Passager, "The Island Is Its Own Gospel"

Persimmon Tree, "The Final Leaves" (now "Learning to Read")

Pine Mountain Sand & Gravel, "Murmuration of Starlings," "To See Small Fish in High Branches"

Psaltery & Lyre, "Surface Tension"

River Heron Review, "Leavings"

Roanoke Review, "Résistance"

Rockvale Review, "What Rope Is For"
Sheila-Na-Gig, "The Mind's Ether," "Prodigal Father"
Sky Island Journal, "Figure of Song"
SPANK the CARP, "Straight from the Deeps of Stanley"
SWWIM Every Day, "Crows Call, High Above the Floodplain"
Turtle Island Quarterly, "Charmouth Bay"
Typishly, "Cadence"
Underwood, "Elegy for a Father" (now "Eclipse")
The West Review, "Near Piccadilly"
Writing for Life Anthology (Nervous Ghost Press), "Fog," "Pit and All"
   (now "The Thing Itself"), "Your Desire a Loaded Spring"
A Casting Off (chapbook, Finishing Line Press, May 2019), "The Amphib-
   ious Body," "Birds and Trees, My Mother's Paintings"

Glass Lyre Press

exceptional works to replenish the spirit

Glass Lyre Press is an independent literary publisher interested in technically accomplished, stylistically distinct, and original work. Glass Lyre seeks diverse writers that possess a dynamic aesthetic and an ability to emotionally and intellectually engage a wide audience of readers.

Glass Lyre's vision is to connect the world through language and art. We hope to expand the scope of poetry and short fiction for the general reader through exceptionally well-written books, which evoke emotion, provide insight, and resonate with the human spirit.

Poetry Collections
Poetry Chapbooks
Select Short & Flash Fiction
Anthologies

www.GlassLyrePress.com

Made in the USA
Monee, IL
03 May 2022

95806076R00059